5

Student's Book

Richmond

Richmond

58 St Aldates
Oxford
OX1 1ST
United Kingdom

Beep Student's Book / Activity Book Level 5

First Edition: 2014
Eighteenth Reprint: 2023
ISBN: 978-607-06-0941-1

© Text: Brendan Dunne, Robin Newton
© Richmond Publishing, S.A. de C.V. 2014
Av. Río Mixcoac No. 274, Col. Acacias,
Benito Juárez, C.P. 03240, Ciudad de México

Publisher: Justine Piekarowicz
Editorial Team: Griselda Cacho, Rodrigo Caudillo, Diane Hermanson
Art and Design Coordinator: Marisela Pérez
Pre-Press Coordinator: Daniel Santillán

Illustrations: Inés Burgos Pía, Ángeles Peinador Arbiza, Álex Orbe, Pablo Velarde Díaz-Pache, Alberto Hoyos, *Beehive illustration:* Moreno Chiacchiera, Victor Tavares; *JHS Studio:* Alex Redondo, Carolina Temprado Battad.

Photographs: *A. Real; Atmán Víctor; B. Cobeta; C. Contreras; C. Díez Polanco; C. Jiménez/photoAlquimia; C. Pérez; D. López; D. Sanchez; C. Suárez; E. Artiles; E. Marín; F. M. Guillén; GARCÍA-PELAYO/Juancho; I. Meléndez; I. Rovira; J. C. Muñoz; J. Escandell.com; J. I. Medina; J. Jaime/ END-PC; J. Lucas; J. M.ª Escudero/ Instituto Municipal de Deportes de Madrid; J. Rosselló; J. Zorita; J. V. Resino; L. Agromayor; L. Gallo; M. San Félix; M. Sánchez; O. Boé; KAIBIDE DE CARLOS FOTÓGRAFOS; M. G. Vicente; Michele di Piccione; O. Torres; ORONOZ; Prats i Camps; S. Enríquez; S. Padura; X. S. Lobato; A. G. E. FOTOSTOCK/ David B. Fleetham, Tomás Abad; Reinhard Dirscherl, Paolo Siccardi; BananaStock, José Peral, Herbert Hopfensperger; ALBUM/ akg-images, Joan Reig/Prisma; CENTRAL STOCK; COMSTOCK; CORDON PRESS/CORBIS/Chistopher Felver; DIGITAL BANK; DIGITALVISION; EFE/ André kertész Andor, Dennis M. Sabangan, EPA/M, Armin Weigel. A. Pushpa Kumara, EFE/SIPA-PRESS/ Dalmas, SIPA ICONO / Patrick Morin; Frederico Mendes; ESTUDIO FOTOGRÁFICO SISSY/M. Arrazola; FOCOLTONE; GETTY IMAGES SALES SPAIN/ Thinkstock/Monkey Business Images Ltd., Thinkstock/ Edgardo Contreras, Thinkstock/Design Pics/Robert Cable, Thinkstock/ Brand X Pictures, Thinkstock/Jupiterimages, Thinkstock/Chris Amaral, Photos.com Plus, Thinkstock; HIGHRES PRESS STOCK AbleStock.com; I. PREYSLER; J. M.ª BARRES; JOHN FOXX IMAGES; SEIS X SEIS; NASA; PHOTODISC; STOCK PHOTOS; Rafa Arroyo Muñoz; J. Carli; MATTON-BILD; MUSEO NUMISMÁTICO, ATENAS; Samsung; SERIDEC PHOTOIMAGENES CD/ PHOTOALTO; Image Source Limited, ARCHIVO SANTILLANA*

Cover Design: Leandro Pauloni
Cover Photograph: THINKSTOCK; iStock, *Ammit*

All rights reserved. No part of this work may be reproduced, stored in a retrieval system or transmitted in any form or by any means without prior written permission from the Publisher.

Richmond publications may contain links to third party websites or apps. We have no control over the content of these websites or apps, which may change frequently, and we are not responsible for the content or the way it may be used with our materials. Teachers and students are advised to exercise discretion when accessing the links.

The Publisher has made every effort to trace the owner of copyright material; however, the Publisher will correct any involuntary omission at the earliest opportunity.

First published by Richmond Publishing / Santillana Educación S.L.

Printed in Brazil by Forma Certa Gráfica Digital
Lote: 796877
Cod: 292709411
2024

Contents

0	Hello!	2
1	Home Time	5
2	Kids can cook!	13
3	Staying Healthy!	21
	Review 1	29

4	Let's go shopping!	33
5	Ocean Life	41
6	Wonderful World	49
	Review 2	57

7	A great day!	61
8	Adventure Island	69
	Review 3	77

Hello!

LESSON 1

1 Read, then listen and guess the name.

Name: Anita
Family: a brother
Eyes: brown
Birthday: March
Pets: no pets
Favorite Subject: science

Name: Kim
Family: only child
Eyes: brown
Birthday: October
Pets: a dog
Favorite Subject: art

Name: Ben
Family: two sisters
Eyes: blue
Birthday: June
Pets: a cat
Favorite Subject: IT

Name: Mark
Family: a sister
Eyes: brown
Birthday: December
Pets: a hamster
Favorite Subject: PE

2 Play a game.

My birthday's in October and my favorite subject is art.

Are you Kim?

Yes, I am!

3 Ask a friend.

Do you have any brothers or sisters?

What color are your eyes?

When's your birthday?

Do you have any pets?

What's your favorite subject?

LESSON 2

 Listen and sing.

My name's Mark!
How are you?
These are the things I like to do.
I like swimming in the sea,
And watching cartoons on TV.

My name's Kim!
How are you?
These are the things I like to do.
I like going to the zoo,
Taking photos and painting, too.

My name's Anita!
How are you?
These are the things I like to do.
Playing basketball at the gym,
And singing songs with my friend Kim.

My name's Ben!
How are you?
These are the things I like to do.
Rollerblading in the park,
And playing games with my friend Mark.

 Read and answer. Write about you.

Hi!
My name's Ellen. I'm ten years old.
I like going to the movies and playing basketball with my friends. At home, I like playing computer games and gardening.
I don't like drawing or painting.
My favorite activity is reading!

Hello!
My name's Declan. I'm ten years old.
I like going to the swimming pool and playing cards with my friends.
At home, I like playing computer games and making models. I don't like playing basketball or painting.
My favorite activity is singing!

LESSON 3

6 Find and name.

- THREE SPORTS
- FOUR NUMBERS
- THREE STORY CHARACTERS
- THREE SCHOOL SUBJECTS
- FOUR SPACE WORDS
- THREE SUMMER ACTIVITIES

7 Listen and say the word.

1. Home Time

LESSON 1

1 Listen and sing. 1.1

When I come home from school,
So many things to do.
I walk the dog,
I clean my room,
I do my homework, too.

I practice the recorder,
I sometimes see my friends,
I have my dinner and do the dishes,
And go to bed at ten.

I love to be at home,
It's my favorite place.
Whenever I'm at home,
There's a smile on my face!

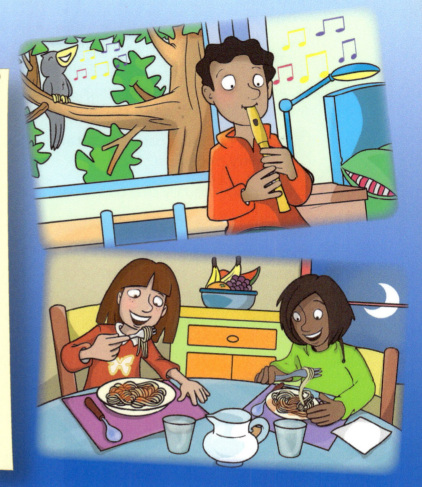

2 Listen and choose the picture. 1.2

 clean my room	 have dinner	 do the dishes	 walk the dog
 see my friends	 practice the recorder	 do my homework	 go to bed

LESSON 2

3 Listen and read.

> Ben and Anita are walking home from school.

 Hi, Anita! I see you have a recorder. **Do you practice the recorder every day?**

 Yes, I usually practice after school in my bedroom.

 That's good. I usually play basketball after school.

 Do you see your friends, too?

 Yes, I sometimes see my friends. We play computer games or listen to music.

 Oh really? My friends all like music, too! What time do you have dinner?

 I always have dinner at six thirty.

 That's early! And do you go to bed at seven o'clock?

 No! I never go to bed at seven o'clock. I go to bed at nine thirty.

 Me too! This is my house. Bye, Ben

 See you tomorrow!

4 Look and read. Which sentence is in the dialogue?

I	always	walk the dog.
	usually	go to bed at nine o'clock.
	sometimes	see my friends.
	never	practice the recorder.

always					
usually					
sometimes					
never					

5 Read about Paul. Write about your evenings.

In the Evening
I usually do my homework at six o'clock and I always have dinner with my family at seven o'clock. After dinner, I sometimes do the dishes. Then I usually play computer games in my room. I sometimes watch TV at nine o'clock and I sometimes read comics with my sister. I usually go to bed at ten o'clock.

LESSON 3

6 Listen and say the name.

7 Ask a friend about their evenings.

The Science Project!

LESSON 4

8 Read and listen to the story.

Ron takes his helmet off. It's time to go home. **5**

Buster is behind a bush. What's he doing? **6**

Buster is digging up dinosaur bones! **7**

Ron's teacher is very happy with his homework, and so is Ron! **8**

LESSON 5

9 Listen and repeat the chant.

I usually get up at quarter to eight,
I'm never late for school.
I sometimes have science at ten fifteen,
Science is really cool!

I have my lunch at one o'clock,
And then I play with my friends.
I finish school at quarter to five,
And then I go home again!

10 Look and say the times in pairs.

It's six fifteen.

The red clock!

11 Ask a friend.

1 What time do you get up?
2 What time do you have science?
3 What time do you have lunch?
4 What time do you do your homework?
5 What time do you have dinner?
6 What time do you go to bed?

What time do you get up?

I usually get up at seven fifteen.

CLIL

LESSON 6

2 Read and answer *True* or *False*.

1 Dogs need a lot of exercise. We walk our dog twice a day. My dad always walks her in the morning and I usually walk her in the park after school. She likes running and playing ball games.

2 Dogs drink a lot of water. I always give my dog a bowl of fresh water every day. He always eats in the evening. On Sunday, I sometimes give him dog biscuits for a treat.

3 Dogs can get dirty. I sometimes give my dog a bath on Saturdays. I use a special shampoo for dogs. He likes having a bath!

4 I sometimes take my dog to the vet. He examines her teeth and gives her injections.

3 Do you know?

Hamsters are desert animals. In the desert, they sleep in the day and they wake up at night and look for food.

Hamsters usually live for 2 to 3 years. Rabbits usually live for 5 to 10 years and cats usually live for 10 to 15 years.

Hamsters are omnivores. They eat fruit, plants, seeds and insects.

The Adventures of Beep!

LITERACY

LESSON 7

14 Read and listen.

15 Listen and repeat a tongue twister.

Dom and Tom have dinner together,
Then Dom does the dishes,
And Tom takes out his toys!

2. Kids can cook!

LESSON 1

1 Listen and sing. 2.1

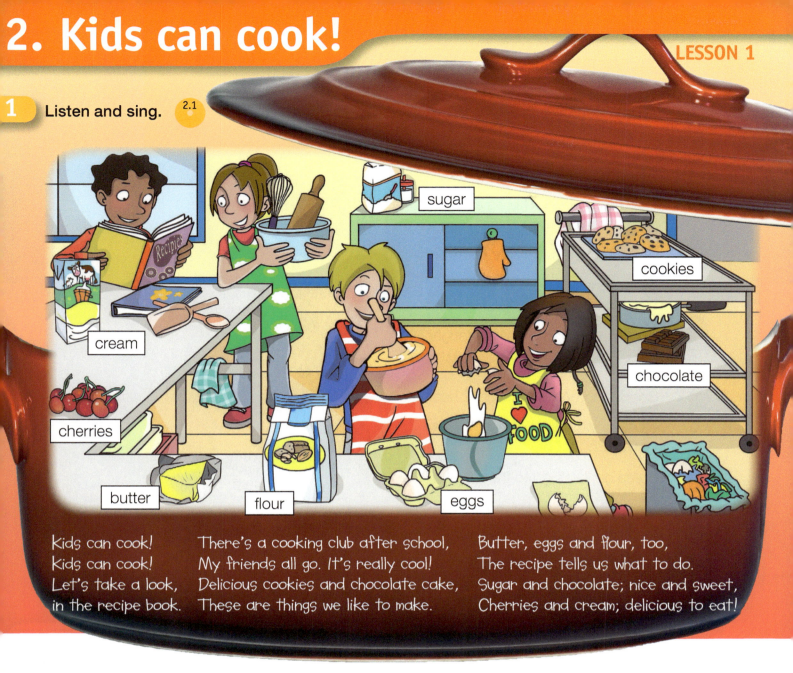

Kids can cook!
Kids can cook!
Let's take a look,
in the recipe book.

There's a cooking club after school,
My friends all go. It's really cool!
Delicious cookies and chocolate cake,
These are things we like to make.

Butter, eggs and flour, too,
The recipe tells us what to do.
Sugar and chocolate; nice and sweet,
Cherries and cream; delicious to eat!

2 Ask and spell.

LESSON 2

3. Listen and read.

> Mark and Kim are writing a shopping list. They want to make chocolate cookies.

 Mark, **do we have any flour?**

 Yes, we do. There's a bag of flour in the cabinet.

 Great! **Do we have any butter?**

 No, we don't, but we have some eggs.

 Good! And do we have any sugar?

 Yes, we have some sugar.

 Good! And do we have any chocolate?

 No, we don't. We don't have any butter or chocolate.

 Come on! Let's go to the store!

 Good idea!

4. Look and read. Which sentence is in the dialogue?

We have	some	cherries.
We don't have	any	cream.

Do we have any butter?	Yes, we do. No, we don't.

5. Look, read and say *the boys* or *the girls*.

We have some cookies. ✓

We don't have any chocolate. ✗

We have some flour. ✓

We have some butter. ✓

We don't have any cream. ✗

We don't have any cherries. ✗

LESSON 3

6 Listen and identify the bags.

7 Copy and complete the diagram for you.

8 Read, then write about you in your notebook.

Hello, I'm Raquel. I'm from Portugal.
I have breakfast with my brother. We always have cereal and orange juice.
I have lunch at school with my friends. We usually have chicken, pasta or fish. Pasta is my favorite food. I like pasta with meat or tomato sauce.
I have a snack at five o'clock. I always have fruit.
I have dinner with my mom, dad and brother. We usually have soup or rice and vegetables.

Kids Start Cooking!

LESSON 4

9 Read and listen to the story.

Eric and Kate are on the Red Team. Danny and Liz are on the Blue Team.

1

Oh no! Kate is switching the sugar for salt.

2

Kate and Eric put butter and sugar in the bowl and mix them with a spoon.

3

Liz and Danny put eggs and flour into the bowl.

4

Kate! Do we have any chocolate chips?

Yes, here they are!

Look! Eric is taking the wrong bowl! — 5

Now, bake in the oven for twenty minutes.

Ok!

Danny puts the cookies in the oven. — 6

The cookies are ready. But who is the winner?

Ugh! This has lots of salt in it.

What?!

Kate doesn't understand. — 7

Well done, Blue Team!

Kate is angry with Eric. Liz and Danny are the winners! — 8

LESSON 5

10 Listen and repeat the rap.

I'm a famous chef,
You can see me on TV.
I can teach you how to cook,
Just copy me!

What do you want to make today?
Chocolate cookies, please!
OK!

Flour and eggs and some butter,
Chocolate chips and some sugar.

Put the ingredients in a big bowl,
And don't get flour on the remote control!

Mix the ingredients with a spoon,
The cookies will be ready soon.

Bake them in the oven on a metal tray,
Now they're ready shout, *hurray!*

11 Read and match.

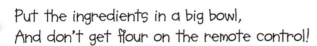

**Recipe:
Chocolate Chip Cookies**
2 eggs
200 grams of butter
300 grams of sugar
300 grams of flour
250 grams of chocolate chips

A Slowly add the flour and mix.
B Add the eggs.
C Put the butter and sugar in a bowl.
D Bake in an oven for 20 minutes.
E Mix the butter and sugar with a fork.
F Add the chocolate chips.

CLIL

LESSON 6

2 Read and name the season.

In the fall, the farmer ploughs a field with a tractor and plants the wheat seeds.

In winter, it's cold and the wheat doesn't grow.

In spring, the wheat grows. Rain and light from the sun help it grow.

In summer, the farmer cuts the wheat with a combine harvester.

The farmer takes the wheat to a mill. Machines make flour from the wheat.

You can buy flour in a grocery store or supermarket and make bread, cookies and cakes.

1 It's cold and the wheat doesn't grow.
2 The farmer cuts the wheat.
3 The farmer plants the wheat seeds.
4 The wheat starts to grow.

3 Do you know?

Cereals, pasta and noodles are all made from wheat.

The world leaders in wheat production are China, India and the USA.

Wheat and rice are types of cereal grain.

The Adventures of Beep!

LITERACY

LESSON 7

14 Read and listen.

15 Listen and repeat a tongue twister.

Ben puts a big piece of butter in a purple bowl to bake some bread.

3. Staying Healthy!

LESSON 1

1 Listen and sing.

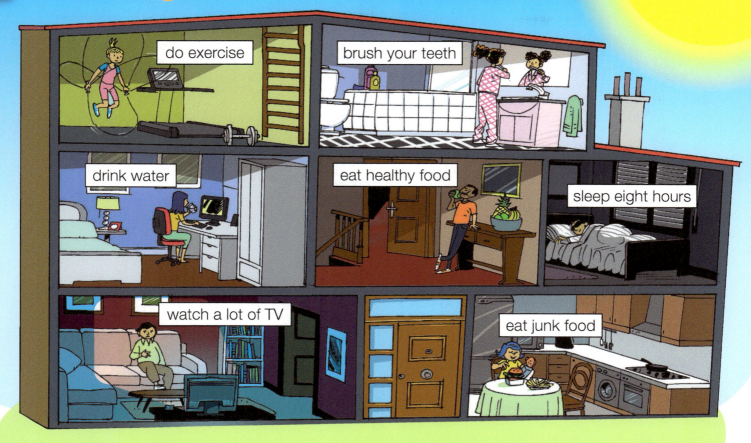

Let's be healthy, let's be strong,
Let's all sing a healthy song.

Do exercise, run, and play,
And always sleep eight hours a day.

Don't be lazy, listen to me!
Please don't watch too much TV.

Eat healthy food every day,
Drink lots of water. That's OK!

Don't eat junk food, don't eat sweets,
Eat fruit and vegetables, fish and meat.

Take a shower, keep clean and bright,
And brush your teeth, day and night.

2 Ask your friends.

How many glasses of water do you drink a day?

How many hours do you sleep at night?

When do you brush your teeth?

Do you do exercise and play sports?

What healthy food do you eat?

I eat a lot of fish, chicken and salad.

LESSON 2

3 Listen and read.

> Kim and Ben are reading a magazine. There's a questionnaire about health.

How often do you do exercise?

Three times a week. I like dancing and swimming.

How often do you watch TV?

I watch TV twice a week.

How often do you eat sweets?

I eat sweets once a week.

How often do you eat fruit?

I eat fruit every day. Do you want an apple?

Yes, thanks, Kim. You're very healthy!

4 Look and read. Which sentence is in the dialogue?

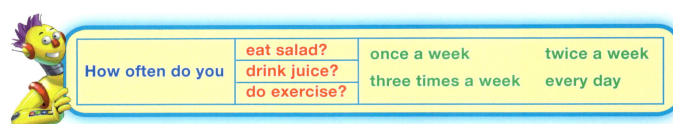

How often do you	eat salad?	once a week	twice a week
	drink juice?	three times a week	every day
	do exercise?		

5 Read the questionnaire and answer.

1 How often do you eat fruit?
   a every day   **b** three times a week   **c** once a week
2 How often do you brush your teeth?
   a once a week   **b** once a day   **c** twice a day
3 How often do you do exercise?
   a once a week   **b** three or four times a week   **c** every day
4 How often do you sleep for eight hours?
   a every day   **b** four or five times a week   **c** twice a week
5 How often do you eat junk food?
   a once a week   **b** three or four times a week   **c** every day

1 a) 3 b) 2 c) 1
2 a) 1 b) 2 c) 3
3 a) 1 b) 2 c) 3
4 a) 3 b) 2 c) 1
5 a) 3 b) 2 c) 1

5-8 Remember, it's important to do exercise and eat healthy food!
9-12 Good! You are healthy but you can do more!
13-15 Excellent! You are very healthy. See you at the Olympics!

LESSON 3

6 Read and answer.

This is Simon. He's from Canada and his hobby is basketball. Simon goes to basketball practice after school four times a week. He goes to the gym twice a week, too, and does exercise. He plays a basketball game with his team once a week. His team is the Toronto Dragons. His ambition is to play basketball in the Olympics.

Simon usually eats healthy food. He has eggs, cereal and fruit for breakfast every day. Once a week, he eats his favorite food. It's cheesecake!

1. How often does Simon go to the gym?
2. How often does he have fruit for breakfast?
3. How often does he eat cheesecake?
4. How often does he go to basketball practice?

7 Read about Irene. Write about your week.

My Week
My name's Irene. I'm from Chile and my hobby is soccer. I go to soccer practice twice a week. I'm on a soccer team and we play a game once a week. My ambition is to play soccer in the Women's World Cup. I like swimming, too, and I go to the swimming pool once a week. I usually eat healthy food and I have fruit every day. I sometimes eat ice cream and pizza, too. I usually sleep nine hours, but on Sundays I sleep twelve hours!

8 Tell a friend the name of…

1. … a show you watch **once a week**.
2. … a sport you practice **twice a week**.
3. … a drink you have **every day**.
4. … a subject you have **twice a week**.
5. … a person you see **every day**.
6. … a website you visit **every day**.

Kay's Big Race!

LESSON 4

9 Read and listen to the story.

This is Kay. She loves sports. She really wants to play soccer...

...but she can't.

1

Kay can't walk, but she can go very fast in her wheelchair AND she can swim. She goes swimming with her friend Dave every day.

2

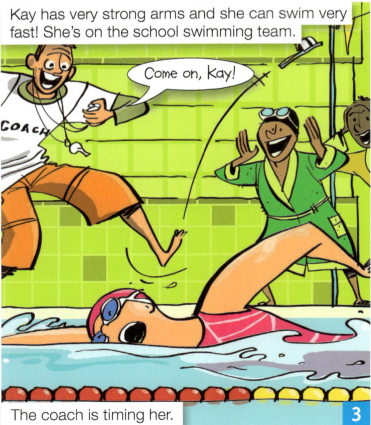

Kay has very strong arms and she can swim very fast! She's on the school swimming team.

Come on, Kay!

The coach is timing her.

3

Kay always has healthy snacks after swimming practice.

Can I have a soft drink?

Sorry, not today. Too much sugar is bad for you.

4

5 Kay and Dave are looking at the bulletin board. "Look, the competition is on Friday." "I hope we win a trophy!" Dave is on the swimming team, too.

6 "Here are your goggles. Good luck, Kay!" "Thanks, Dave!" Kay's race is starting soon. Dave hopes she wins.

7 "Well done, Kay! You're the best!" Kay wins the race. Her friends are very happy, and so is her dad.

8 "I love chocolate cake!" "Sugar is good for you sometimes!" Kay has chocolate cake once a week.

LESSON 5

10 Listen and repeat the chant.

Some things are good for you,
So do them every day.
Eat lots of healthy food,
It helps you work and play.

Get lots of exercise,
And sleep eight hours a night.
Keep your body nice and clean,
It helps you feel all right.

Some things are bad for you,
Don't do them every day.
Don't eat lots of junk food,
If you want to feel OK.

Watching TV's really great,
And sweets and soft drinks.
But too much is bad for you,
So think, think, think!

11 Follow and read.

Eating fruit is good for you because…

Sleeping eight hours is good for you because…

Eating a lot of sweets and candy is bad for you because…

Doing exercise is good for you because…

your body grows at night, when you're sleeping.

it helps your body grow and be strong.

it contains natural sugar and vitamin C for energy and good health.

they contain a lot of sugar and can make you fat.

12 Look and say with a friend.

Sleeping five hours a night.

Drinking water with meals.

Brushing your teeth once a month.

It's good for you. ✓

It's bad for you. ✗

Riding your bike three times a week.

Eating junk food every day.

Taking a shower every day.

CLIL

LESSON 6

3 Read and answer.

> This is a human skeleton. Children have three hundred bones in their skeletons, but adults have two hundred and six. Some bones join together when we grow!

- The skull protects your brain. Babies have soft skulls, but they become hard in the first six months of life.

- Young children have twenty teeth. These teeth fall out when children are six or seven years old. Then they grow thirty-two new teeth.

- We have twelve pairs of ribs. They protect the heart and lungs.

- The spine is a long chain of bones called vertebrae. The spine is in the middle of your back. Children have thirty vertebrae. Some of the vertebrae join together when children grow, and adults have twenty-six vertebrae. The spine is flexible so we can run, dance and touch our toes!

- More than half of the bones in the human body are in the hands and feet. There are twenty-seven bones in each hand.

- There are twenty-six bones in each foot.

How can I have healthy bones?

Do exercise. Running, dancing and playing sports make strong bones!

Eat fruit and vegetables and drink milk. Fruit, vegetables and milk all have calcium in them. Calcium helps bones and teeth grow.

Play outside. Light from the sun makes vitamin D in our skin. We need vitamin D for strong bones.

Wear a helmet. Riding a bike and skateboarding are healthy, but it's important to protect your skull with a helmet.

4 Listen and answer *True* or *False*. 3.5

The Adventures of Beep!

LITERACY

LESSON 7

15 Read and listen.

16 Listen and repeat a tongue twister.

Lonny likes reading and listening to rap, but Ronny likes running long races.

Review 1

1. Name and spell!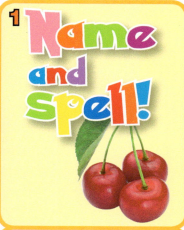
2. Name five healthy foods.
3. Do you brush your teeth twice a day?
4. What time do you have dinner?
8. Name and spell!
7. On Saturday, I sometimes...
6. What time is it?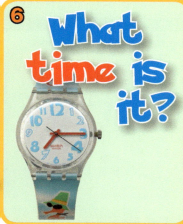
5. How often do you do exercise?
9. Name and spell!
10. How often do you do the dishes?
11. What time is it?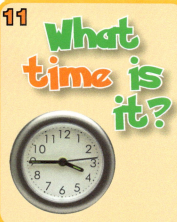
12. Name three unhealthy foods.
16. What time do you go to bed?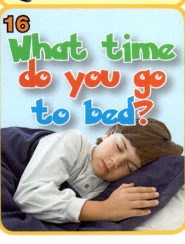
15. How often do you clean your room?
14. Name and spell!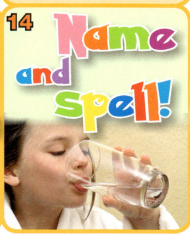
13. In winter, I never...

1 Look and ask a friend.

Always ✓✓✓
Usually ✓✓
Sometimes ✓
Never ✗

- brush your teeth at night
- do exercise on Saturday
- go to the beach in winter
- watch TV in the morning
- do the dishes after dinner
- practice the recorder
- sleep eight hours at night
- do your homework in the kitchen

Do you brush your teeth at night?
Yes, I always brush my teeth at night.

2 Describe a bag to a friend.

Do you have any flour?
No, I don't.
Do you have any chocolate?
Yes, I do.
Bag 4!

3 Read and answer *True* or *False*.

Hi, I'm Scott. On school days, I always get up at seven fifteen. I usually have cereal and orange juice for breakfast. I go to school at eight thirty. At school, my favorite subjects are science and Spanish. I don't like art. Painting and drawing are difficult for me!
I go to soccer practice twice a week after school. I like doing exercise. It's good for you.
I usually have dinner at seven o'clock. I always do the dishes after dinner. Then I sometimes read books and play computer games with my sister.

1 Scott always gets up at seven o'clock.
2 He never has cereal for breakfast.
3 His favorite subjects are math and PE.
4 He doesn't like art.
5 He goes to soccer practice twice a week.
6 He sometimes does the dishes.

4 Write about your day.

4. Let's go shopping!

LESSON 1

1 Listen and sing. 4.1

We're going shopping, Mom and I,
For all the things we need to buy.
Get off the bus and look around,
At all the stores in our town.

A farmers' market and bakery, too,
A supermarket with food for you.
If you need clothes or books or shoes,
There are lots of stores for you to choose.

If you need soccer shirts or shorts,
Then there's a special store for sports.
And look! A new computer store,
Not so far from our door.

We're going shopping, Mom and I,
For all the things we need to buy.

2 Listen and identify. 4.2

1 shoe store

2 farmers' market

3 bookstore

4 supermarket

5 bakery

6 computer store

7 sports store

8 clothing store

LESSON 2

3 Look and read.

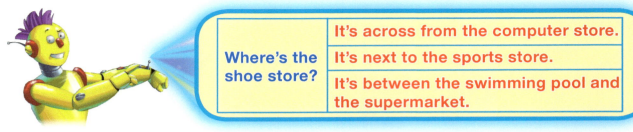

Where's the shoe store?
- It's across from the computer store.
- It's next to the sports store.
- It's between the swimming pool and the supermarket.

4 Look at the icons and identify the place. Then listen and check.

5 Look at the map. Listen and answer *True* or *False*. Then ask a friend. 4.3

Where's the bakery?

It's across from the swimming pool.

34

LESSON 3

6 Listen and read.

> Kim is at a bookstore. She's talking to the salesperson.

 Hello, can I help you?

 Yes, I want to buy a book.

 Good! **Do you like comic books?**

 Yes, I do. I really like comic books. They're funny.

 Do you like information books, too?

 Yes, I like information books about science and dinosaurs.

 What about a joke book? We have lots of joke books.

 No, thank you, I hate joke books. I prefer books with stories.

 What about a novel? Do you like novels?

 Yes, I love novels. Do you have a novel about detectives?

 Yes, I do. Look, this is a novel about a girl detective.

 Oh, fantastic! Can I have this book, please?

 Yes, here you are. It's six dollars.

7 Ask a friend.

1 Do you like reading?
2 How often do you read?
3 What are your favorite books?
4 Is there a bookstore in your town?

8 Read about Gabriel. Write about the books you like.

Hello, I'm Gabriel.
I love reading. I always read in bed at night and I sometimes read in the car, too. I really like novels about children. My favorite novel is *Charlie and the Chocolate Factory*.
I hate novels about ghosts or monsters.
I sometimes read information books, too.
I really like information books about space, science and animals. I love comic books. My favorite comic books are the *Tintin* books.

A Day in London!

9 Read and listen to the story.

The police are chasing the thief but they can't see him.

- Where is he?
- He's turning right!

Danny and his mom look in the bag.

- It's a computer!
- And here's a name. It's P.J. Downing! Let's take it to the bookstore.

P.J. Downing

- My new story is on the computer. It's the only copy!
- We're looking for it now.
- Excuse me, here's your computer.

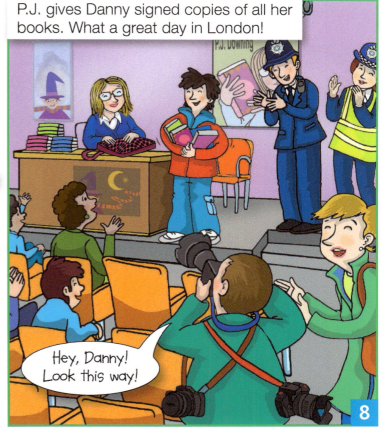

P.J. gives Danny signed copies of all her books. What a great day in London!

- Hey, Danny! Look this way!

LESSON 5

10 Listen and repeat the chant.

Where's the bookstore? Do you know?
Tell me, please, which way to go!

First turn left and then turn right,
Then you see the traffic lights.

Go straight. Go past the school,
Then turn right at the swimming pool.

Turn right again and there's a bus stop,
Next to that you'll see the bookstore.

11 Look, listen and identify the place.

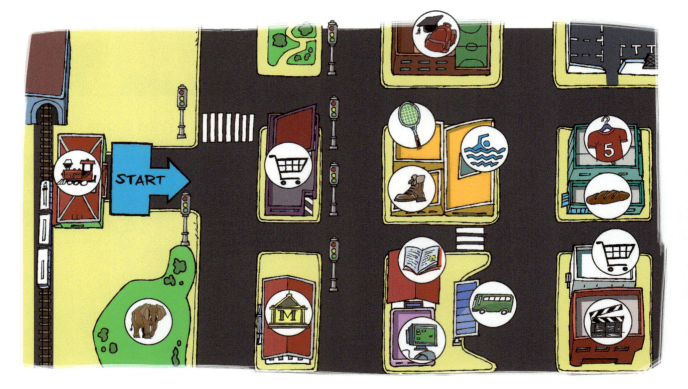

12 Read and say. Play in pairs.

Start at the station and go straight. Turn right at the traffic lights and then turn left. Turn left at the traffic lights. I'm next to the sports store. Where am I?

CLIL

LESSON 6

3 Read and choose the picture.

| Be safe on foot! | Walk quickly. Listen for cars and look left and right when you cross the street. | When you want to cross the street, find a crosswalk or traffic lights. | Wait for the green light. Don't cross the street when the light is red. |

4 Read about bike safety, then look and choose the picture.

1. Ride your bike in a bicycle lane.
2. Wear a helmet to protect your head.
3. Wear colorful clothes and have a colorful bag.
4. Have a bell on your bike.
5. Stop when you see a red light.
6. Have lights and reflectors on your bike.

5 Listen and find the mistakes.

The Adventures of Beep!

LITERACY

LESSON 7

16 Read and listen.

17 Listen and repeat a tongue twister.

Grandma and Grandpa grab some green grapes. They're great!

5. Ocean Life

LESSON 1

1 Listen and sing. 5.1

We're going to the aquarium,
My friends are coming with me,
To learn about the animals,
That live in the sea.

Blue whales, seals and jellyfish,
Orcas, crabs and turtles, too.

Octopuses and great white sharks,
All live in the sea so blue.

We're going to the aquarium,
My friends are coming with me.
To learn about the animals,
That live in the sea.

2 Describe and guess.

It's small and red. It starts with C.

Is it the crab?

Yes, it is!

LESSON 2

3 Listen and read.

> Mark is doing a project on great white sharks. He's talking to a shark expert.

 Hello, can I ask you some questions about great white sharks?

 Yes, of course. What do you want to know?

 Do great white sharks live in groups?

 No, they don't. They live alone.

 Do they eat turtles?

 Yes, they do. They eat turtles, seals and fish.

 Do they lay eggs?

 No, they don't. They have babies.

 Do they breathe air?

 No, they don't. They take oxygen from the water. Do you like great white sharks, Mark?

 Yes, but I don't want to meet one!

 Me neither, but I think they are amazing animals.

 Thanks for talking to me. Now I can write my project.

 You're welcome. Bye!

4 Look and read. Which sentence is in the dialogue?

They	live	alone.
	don't eat	crabs.

Do they eat plants?	Yes, they do. No, they don't.

5 Read and match.

1. They live in groups near to the ocean. They eat fish and they breathe air.

2. They live alone. They eat crabs and small fish. They lay eggs.

3. They live in groups. They eat seals and fish. They don't lay eggs.

A

B

C

LESSON 3

6 Look, listen and name the animal.

		They live in groups.	They breathe air.	They lay eggs.
dolphin		✓	✓	✗
sea horse		✗	✗	✓
turtle		✗	✓	✓
crab		✓	✗	✓

What are these animals? They don't live in groups. They don't breathe air. They lay eggs.

7 Take the ocean animals quiz. Then listen and check. 5.3

1. Do starfish live in groups?
2. Do seals lay eggs?
3. Do jellyfish eat plants?
4. Do sharks breathe air?
5. Do dolphins eat plants?
6. Do orcas live in groups?
7. Do crabs walk?
8. Do blue whales eat dolphins?

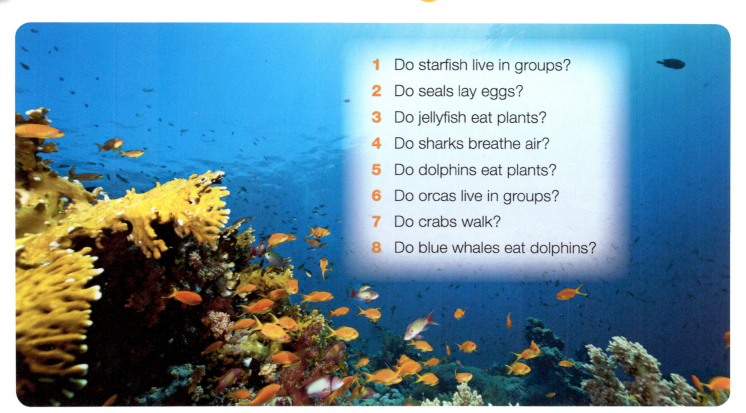

The Shipwreck!

LESSON 4

8 Read and listen to the story.

Karen's mom is a marine biologist. She goes diving with Karen. They see lots of amazing ocean animals.

Can you hear me?

Yes! We're ready to go.

1

They look at the jellyfish. They have long tentacles.

Don't touch the tentacles. They're poisonous.

2

Karen is looking at an octopus. They live on the ocean floor. They have gills and they eat crabs.

Oh no! Poor crab!

Octopuses have arms, not tentacles!

3

Karen is frightened. She can see a big shark. They swim fast and they're dangerous.

Mom! Look!

Quick! Let's hide behind the rocks!

4

Karen and her mom hide from the shark. Karen finds something interesting. She calls her mom.

Mom! It's a shipwreck. Can we look inside?

They are inside the ship. It's very dark. Karen is looking in a box. There are old coins inside.

Mom, look! Treasure!

There are lots of old coins on the ship. They are taking them to a museum.

OK, captain! We have the treasure!

The coins are in the museum. Lots of people come to see them. Karen and her mom are famous now.

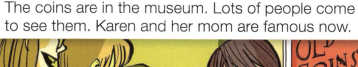

The coins are 500 years old.

LESSON 5

9 Listen and find.

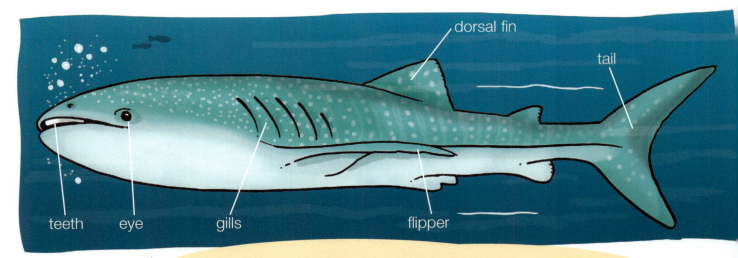

Sharks, fish and octopuses have gills. Gills take oxygen from the water. Dolphins and whales don't have gills. They breathe air.

10 Read and name the animals.

They don't have gills. They have big teeth and a dorsal fin.

They don't have a tail or flippers. They have gills.

11 Listen and sing.

Let's sing the song of the great blue whale.
They swim in the ocean and they have big tails.
They all breathe air.
No, they don't have gills.
They don't have teeth but they all eat krill.
They're very, very big, 30 meters long.
They swim in the ocean and they sing a whale song.

The great blue whale, the great blue whale,
Let's sing the song of the great blue whale.

46

CLIL

LESSON 6

2 Read. Then listen and answer *True* or *False*.

1 The sea turtle swims to the beach.
2 She makes a hole in the sand with her flippers. She lays eggs in the hole.
3 The eggs are white spheres, the size of a table tennis ball.
4 The turtle puts sand on the eggs. She doesn't stay with the eggs. She goes back to the ocean.
5 After six weeks, the baby turtles (or hatchlings) come out of the eggs.
6 The hatchlings climb out of the hole at night. Then they go to the ocean.
7 The hatchlings swim in the ocean. They eat fish and ocean plants.

3 Do you know?

Crabs and birds try to eat the hatchlings!

Turtles can live up to 100 years!

Sea turtles can't put their heads and flippers inside their shells.

The Adventures of Beep!

LITERACY

LESSON 7

14 Read and listen.

15 Listen and repeat a tongue twister.

Sharon and Sheena swimming in the sea,
Sharon sees a shark,
But Sheena sees a ship.
Phew!

6. Wonderful World

LESSON 1

1 Listen and sing.

Look at our world,
Floating in space,
All blue and green,
It's a beautiful place.

There are high, high mountains,
Islands and seas,
Long, long rivers,
And tall, tall trees.

Wide, wide oceans,
And deserts so dry,
Hot volcanoes,
Reach up to the sky.

Big green forests,
And lakes so blue,
Thousands of plants,
And animals, too.

Floating in space,
So all alone,
It's a wonderful world,
And it's our home!

2 Describe and identify in pairs.

1. mountain
2. island
3. river
4. ocean
5. desert
6. volcano
7. forest
8. lake

She's wearing a yellow T-shirt. She's drinking water.

He's wearing a blue coat. He's reading a map.

Picture 6, the volcano!

Picture 7, the forest!

LESSON 2

3 Read and listen. Then look at the numbers and say them.

The Amazon is a river in South America. It is 6,400 kilometers long. A lot of animals live in the river. There are river dolphins, crabs and 2,100 different species of fish.

Teide is a volcano in the Canary Islands in Spain. It is 3,718 meters high. You can take a cable car to near the top. Every year, two million people visit Teide.

The Sahara Desert in Africa is 5,600 kilometers wide. It's about the size of the USA. It's very hot and dry. Sometimes, there is only one millimeter of rain in a year.

Lake Superior is a big lake between Canada and the USA. It is 563 kilometers long and 406 meters deep. It is 10,000 years old. In winter, it is very cold, but you can swim in Lake Superior in the summer.

```
  5,600
2,100    3,718
  563    6,400
  2,000,000
```

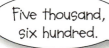 Five thousand, six hundred.

The Sahara Desert is five thousand, six hundred kilometers wide.

4 Read and answer. Write about amazing places in your country.

Amazing Places in France

Mont Blanc is a high mountain in France. There is always snow at the top. Mont Blanc means white mountain in French. It is 4,810 meters high. You can go climbing and hiking on Mont Blanc. Every year, 20,000 people climb to the top.

The Eiffel Tower is in Paris, the capital city of France. It is 324 meters high and it has 1,665 steps. When it's sunny, you can see 60 kilometers from the top. There are two restaurants in the Eiffel Tower. You can have lunch and take photos.

What can you do on Mont Blanc?

What can you do in the Eiffel Tower?

LESSON 3

5 Listen and read.

Mark and Anita are taking a geography quiz.
They're holding question cards and looking at a world map.

 I have a question for you Anita! **The Nile river is longer than the Amazon river.** True or false?

 I think it's true.

 Yes, you're right. **The Nile river is 200 kilometers longer.**

 Now, here's a question about oceans. The Pacific Ocean is bigger than the Indian Ocean. True or false?

 I think it's true. The Pacific Ocean is very big. It's bigger than the Indian Ocean.

 Yes, that's right. Now, I have a question about mountains. Teide is higher than Mont Blanc. True or false?

 It's false, Mont Blanc is higher than Teide. But I don't like that question! Teide isn't a mountain, it's a volcano!

 Oh, Mark! Volcanos are mountains!

6 Look and read. Which sentence is in the dialogue?

Everest is **higher** than Mont Blanc.

The Nile river is **longer** than the Amazon river.

The Pacific Ocean is **bigger** than the Atlantic Ocean.

Remember!
big → bi**gg**er

7 Take the quiz. Listen and check.

1 The volcano Teide is higher than the volcano Etna.
2 South America is bigger than Africa.
3 The Indian Ocean is smaller than the Atlantic Ocean.
4 The Andes Mountains are higher than the Himalaya Mountains.
5 The Ebro river in Spain is longer than the Seine river in France.
6 The North Pole is colder than the South Pole.
7 The Sahara Desert is hotter than the Gobi Desert.
8 Brazil is bigger than Canada.

51

A Long Way to School!

LESSON 4

8 Read and listen to the story.

Tenzin and Nima are from Tibet. They live in a small village high in the mountains. It's windy in the village and they like flying kites. In the winter it's cold and snowy and they can't go to school.

In the spring, Dad takes them to school in the town. It's a long trip. They live in the town until summer.

"Put your gloves on, Nima!"

"Good-bye, Mom!"

The village is 4,845 meters high. It's a lot higher than the town. The trip is dangerous.

"Put your foot here!"

"Be careful, Nima!"

The weather is hotter this year and the ice has melted earlier than usual.

"Oh no! We can't cross the river."

"What can we do now?"

Dad knows a bridge but it's very dangerous. Tenzin goes first. Dad helps the children cross.

5

Tenzin falls, but Dad catches him.

Now, Nima is really scared. She doesn't like the bridge.

6

Everyone crosses the river safely. Now the weather is sunnier.

7

The town is bigger and noisier than the village, but they love going to school.

8

LESSON 5

9 Listen and repeat the chant.

My village in the mountains,
Is quieter than the town.
It's smaller and it's cleaner,
There are flowers all around.

The weather's very different, too,
It's colder there at night.
It's snowier and windier,
But I can fly my kite.

It's hotter and it's sunnier,
When we go to town.
But it's bigger and it's noisier,
With people all around.

10 Look and say in pairs.

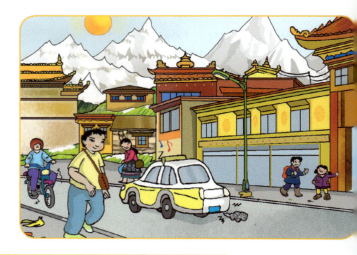

sunny   big   hot   windy   quiet   noisy   clean   cold

The town is sunnier than the village.

sunny ➡ sunn**ier**
noisy ➡ nois**ier**

11 Read and answer *True* or *False*.

1 The village is cloudier than the town.
2 The town is cleaner than the village.
3 The town is noisier than the village.
4 The village is quieter than the town.

CLIL

LESSON 6

2 Listen and say the missing word.

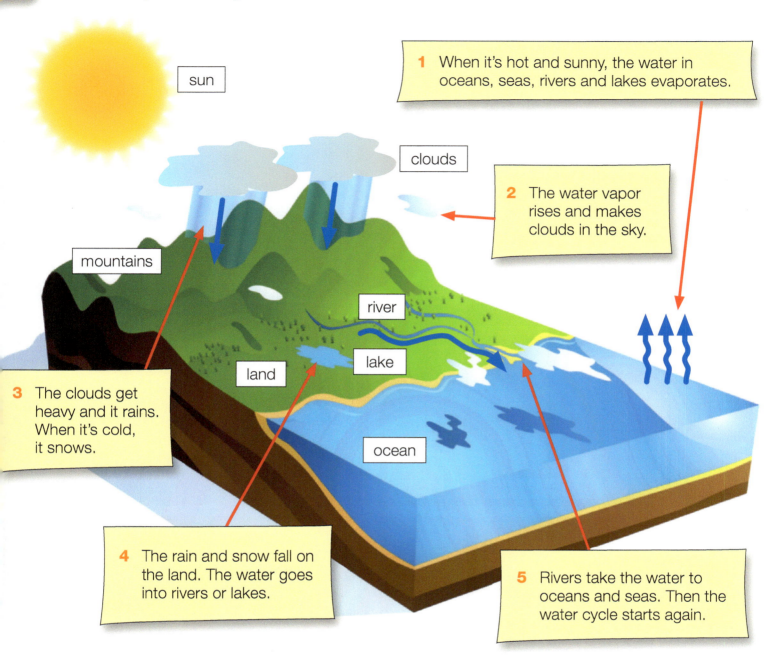

1 When it's hot and sunny, the water in oceans, seas, rivers and lakes evaporates.

2 The water vapor rises and makes clouds in the sky.

3 The clouds get heavy and it rains. When it's cold, it snows.

4 The rain and snow fall on the land. The water goes into rivers or lakes.

5 Rivers take the water to oceans and seas. Then the water cycle starts again.

3 Do you know?

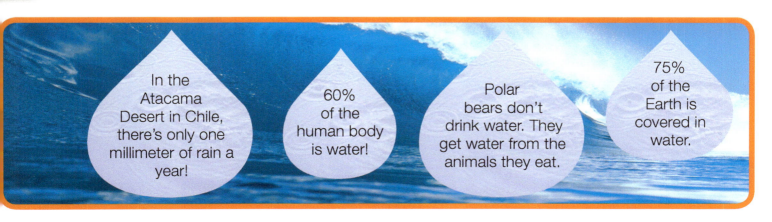

In the Atacama Desert in Chile, there's only one millimeter of rain a year!

60% of the human body is water!

Polar bears don't drink water. They get water from the animals they eat.

75% of the Earth is covered in water.

The Adventures of Beep!

LITERACY

LESSON 7

14 Read and listen.

15 Listen and repeat a tongue twister.

Three fat, funny thieves
find four thousand fish.

Review 2

1 Where do you buy bread?

2 Name and Spell!

3 Do sharks live in groups?

4 Name and Spell!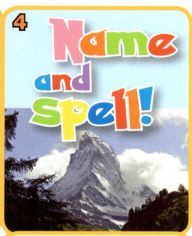

8 10,688 Say!

7 Name and Spell!

6 4,365 Say!

5 Name and Spell!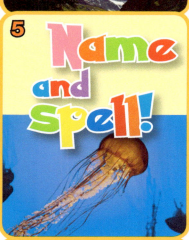

9 Name and Spell!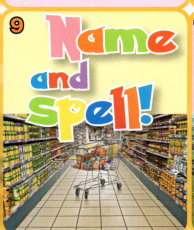

10 Name and Spell!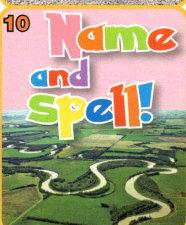

11 Where can you buy jeans?

12 974 Say!

16 Where can you buy novels?

15 Do turtles lay eggs?

14 Name and Spell!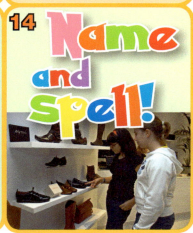

13 Name and Spell!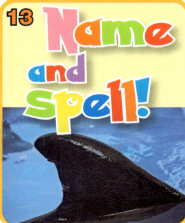

1 Look and ask a friend.

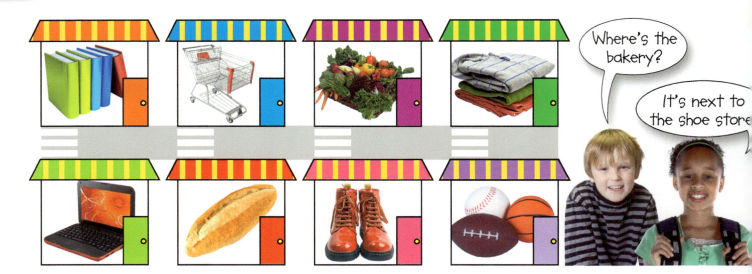

2 Read and name the animals.

What are they?

1 They don't have gills. They breathe air. They're 30 meters long and they eat krill. They can sing!
2 They breathe air and can live on the land and in the ocean. They eat fish and they live in groups.
3 They live alone on the ocean floor. They eat crabs and small fish. They have gills and they lay eggs. They have eight arms.

3 Read and answer *True* or *False*.

Russia is 10.6 million square kilometers.

Lake Superior in Canada is 406 meters deep.

The Thames river is 344 kilometers long.

Mallorca is 3,640 square kilometers.

In the Sahara Desert it can be 57° centigrade.

The USA is 6 million square kilometers.

Mount Teide is 3,718 meters high.

Tenerife is 2,034 square kilometers.

The Ebro river in Spain is 930 kilometers long.

In the Gobi Desert it can be 50° centigrade.

Lake Como in Italy is 410 meters deep.

Mont Blanc is 4,810 meters high.

1 Mount Teide is higher than Mont Blanc.
2 The Sahara desert is hotter than the Gobi desert.
3 The Thames river is longer than the Ebro river.
4 The USA is bigger than Russia.
5 Lake Como is deeper than Lake Superior.
6 Mallorca is smaller than Tenerife.

7. A great day!

LESSON 1

1 Listen and sing. 7.1

I love going out with my family,
We take lots of photos of the things we see.
Here's the aquarium and the planetarium,
And this is the palace. Look, it's me!

So many places we like to go,
An amusement park and a movie studio.
We really like going to a gallery,
Look! That's a painting by Dalí!

Here's another photo with my sister May,
At the skating rink on Saturday.
And here's the bowling alley. Yes, that's me!
I love going out with my family.

2 Look and ask in pairs.

Where's the amusement park?

It's between the movie studio and the planetarium.

1	skating rink	**5**	aquarium
2	movie studio	**6**	bowling alley
3	amusement park	**7**	gallery
4	planetarium	**8**	palace

61

LESSON 2

3 Read and listen.

> Anita and Kim are looking at photos on the computer.

 Look at this photo. **I was at a bowling alley with my brother.**

 How old were you?

 I was eight and my brother was ten.

 I like this photo of the amusement park.

 Me too! I was really excited. Look at my dad! He was scared.

 Is this you at the beach?

 Yes, I was with my mom.

 Was it hot?

 Yes, it was very hot and sunny. It was summer.

 Come on, let's go and take some photos!

 Good idea!

4 Look and read. Which sentence is in the dialogue?

I	was	at a bowling alley.
He/She	was	eleven.
It	was	winter.

How old **were** you?
Where **were** you?

5 Look and say in pairs.

 Ben
 Kim
 Mark
 Anita
 Ruth
 Colin

It was summer. I was at an amusement park.

Are you Ruth?

Yes, I am!

LESSON 3

6 Listen and answer *True* or *False*.

7 Ask a friend.

1 What was your favorite toy?
2 What was your favorite color?
3 Who was your first teacher?
4 What was your favorite food?
5 What was your favorite ice cream flavor?
6 What was your favorite place?
7 What was your favorite TV show?

8 Read and write about you.

When I Was Little
By Megan

When I was little, my favorite food was spaghetti and my favorite drink was milk. My favorite toy was my bike. It was red and white. My favorite place was the park and my favorite game was hide and seek.
At school, Naomi was my teacher and I was in the Dolphins class. My favorite book was a story about elephants. My favorite subject was art.

Robbery at the Palace!

9 Read and listen to the story.

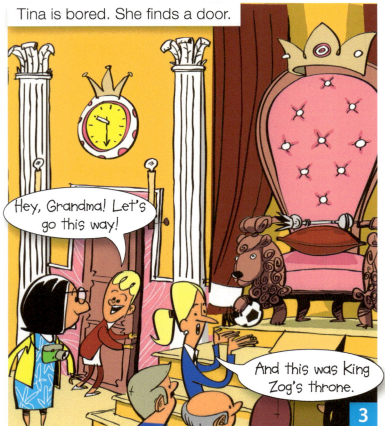

LESSON 5

10 Listen and repeat the chant.

Where were you at five to eight?
I was at the movie theater with my friend Kate.

Where were you at three thirty?
I was with my grandma at the gallery.

Where were you at ten to one?
At the bowling alley with my friend Ron.

Where were you at ten after two?
I was at the amusement park.
How about you?

11 Play the game. Ask and answer in pairs.

Where were you at twenty after eight?

I was at the bowling alley.

CLIL

LESSON 6

2 Read, then answer *True* or *False*.

Welcome to the gallery. Here are some famous artists from the twentieth century.

Pablo Picasso (1881–1973)
Pablo Picasso was from Spain. When he was a baby, his first word was pencil. He was famous for his colorful and unusual paintings of people. His father was an artist, too.

Piet Mondrian (1872–1944)
Piet Mondrian was from Holland. He was from a family of artists. His father was an art teacher. His paintings only have five colors: black, white, yellow, red and blue. They have a lot of black lines and colored rectangles.

Georgia O'Keeffe (1887–1986)
Georgia O'Keeffe was from the USA. She was from a big family. At school, her favorite subject was art. Her favorite place was the desert. Her paintings show the deserts and mountains of the USA.

Eduardo Chillida (1924–2002)
Eduardo Chillida was from Spain. When he was young, his favorite sport was soccer. He was a famous soccer player and an artist. Look at this sculpture by Chillida. It's made of metal. It isn't in a gallery. It's on rocks next to the ocean in San Sebastian in Spain.

3 Ask a friend.

1 Do you like art?

2 Is there a gallery in your town or city?

3 Do you like the paintings and sculpture on this page?

4 Do you know the names of more artists?

67

The Adventures of Beep!

LITERACY

LESSON 7

14 Read and listen. 7.6

15 Listen and repeat a tongue twister. 7.7

Where was Sarah?
Where was Claire?
Where were Blair and Mary?
They were at the aquarium!
The sharks were really scary.

8. Adventure Island

LESSON 1

1 Listen and sing. 8.1

Adventure Island, lost at sea,
Is such a brilliant place to be.
Is there treasure buried there?
Can we find it if we dare?

Anita, Mark, Kim and Ben,
Are on the island, once again.
They want to go to Black Beard's Bay,
But nobody can find the way.

There's the path out of town,
But there's danger all around!
The Cliffs of Death, a waterfall,
A scary bridge, look out! Don't fall!

Around the swamp and through the caves,
Then we hear the ocean waves.
If there's treasure buried there,
We can find it! But beware!

2 Look and ask in pairs.

1
2
3
4
5
6
7
8

1	bay	5	bridge
2	path	6	swamp
3	cliff	7	cave
4	waterfall	8	town

How do you spell "swamp"?

S-W-A-M-P.

Can you see a swamp in the picture in Activity 1?

No, I can't.

69

LESSON 2

3 Read the beginning of the adventure and answer.

Anita, Mark, Ben and Kim are on vacation on Adventure Island. It's a beautiful and exciting place with caves, waterfalls, swamps and a volcano.

On the first day, the children are having breakfast in a café. They're making plans. Anita likes volcanos. She wants to go hiking. Mark likes water sports. He wants to go surfing. Ben likes relaxing.
He wants to go to the beach. Kim likes adventures. She wants to explore the island and look for treasure.

There are a man and a woman having breakfast in the café, too. When they finish eating, they get up and go. But look! Their bag is under the table. Kim is curious. Where did the man and woman go? And what is in the bag?

4 Listen and read. 8.2

Where are the man and woman now?

I don't know. Let's look in the bag for a name or a phone number.

I can't see a name, but there are lots of papers in here.

Look! This one says *Top Secret*.

And look at this map of the island! Who are those people?

I think they're spies… or treasure hunters!

Mark, what do the papers say?

I think they're instructions for finding treasure!

And there are some instructions here. They say **Go through the town and over the bridge.**

Then they say **Go around the swamp, along the cliff and under the waterfall.**

That's impossible! There isn't any treasure. That's only in stories.

Yes, there is! Come on, let's take the map and papers. We can find the treasure!

Good idea, let's go!

Wait! I'm coming, too!

LESSON 3

5 Listen and repeat.

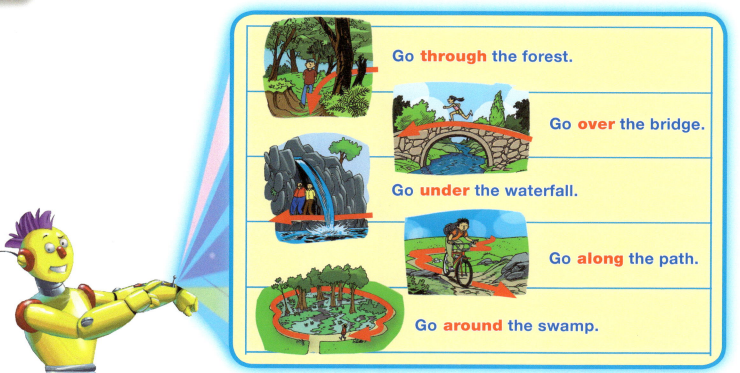

Go **through** the forest.

Go **over** the bridge.

Go **under** the waterfall.

Go **along** the path.

Go **around** the swamp.

6 Look at the map. Listen and follow the directions. 8.3

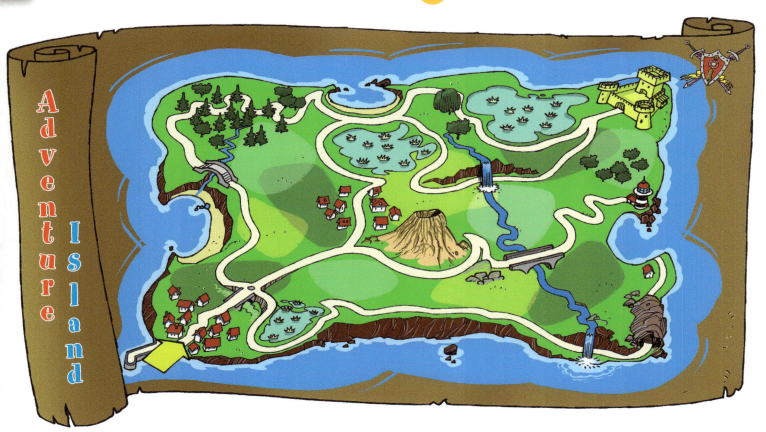

7 Give directions in pairs.

71

The Secret of Blackbeard's Bay!

8 Read and listen to the story.

LESSON 5

9 Listen and repeat the chant.

North, south, east, west,
Looking for a treasure chest.
North or south – we don't know,
East or west – which way to go?
Here's the map. Can you see?
Read the clues and follow me!

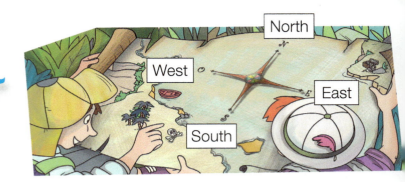

10 Find treasure in pairs.

Start at the castle. Go four squares south. Go one square west. Where's the treasure?

It's behind the waterfall.

11 Read and write a postcard to a friend.

Hi Micky,
I'm on vacation at the beach with my family. I'm having a fantastic time. It's hot and sunny here. I wear shorts and a T-shirt every day. In the morning, I swim in the ocean and go snorkeling. In the afternoon, I read books and ride my bike with my sister. There's a high cliff and a lighthouse here.

See you soon! Andy

CLIL

LESSON 6

2 Listen, read and complete.

cave roof

cave floor

Stalactites
Stalactites hang from the roofs of caves. Water passes through the cave and leaves minerals on the cave roof. Over thousands of years, the minerals grow down and form a stalactite.

Stalagmites
Stalagmites grow from the floor of caves. Water falls from the roof and leaves minerals on the cave floor. Over thousands of years, the minerals grow upward and form a stalagmite.

Columns
Sometimes stalactites and stalagmites join and make a column.

3 Read about bats.

Do bats live in caves?
Bats sometimes live in caves. Bats live in big groups. Sometimes, thousands of bats live in the same cave! They live in forests and deserts, too.

When do bats sleep?
Bats usually sleep in the day and wake up at night. Bats use their claws to sleep upside down.

What do bats eat?
Bats eat fruit and insects. Some big bats eat small animals, too. Bats eat a lot. They can eat half their body weight in one day!

What is echolocation?
When they fly through a cave, bats make sounds. The sounds echo from the cave walls. The echoes help the bats find their way. This is called echolocation. Bats have eyes too but they can't see in the caves when it's dark.

4 Listen and answer *True* or *False*. 8.6

The Adventures of Beep!

LITERACY

LESSON 7

15 Read and listen.

16 Listen and repeat a tongue twister.

Kim climbs a cliff,
Dives in the river,
Finds a big fish,
It's time for dinner!

Review 3

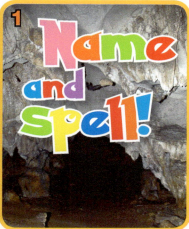
1 Name and spell!

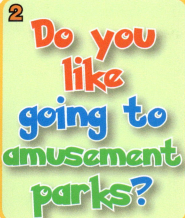
2 Do you like going to amusement parks?

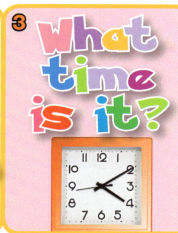
3 What time is it?

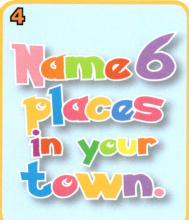
4 Name 6 places in your town.

8 Name 5 aquarium animals.

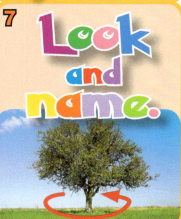
7 Look and name.

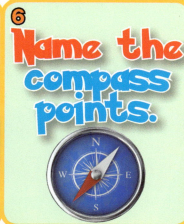
6 Name the compass points.

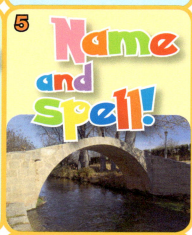
5 Name and spell!

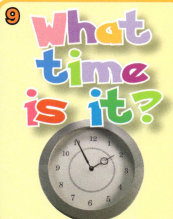
9 What time is it?

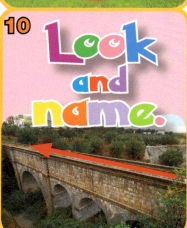
10 Look and name.

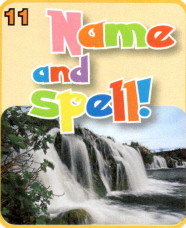
11 Name and spell!

12 Name 2 famous artists.

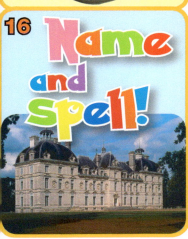
16 Name and spell!

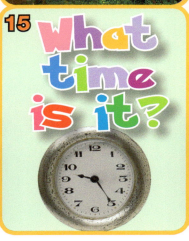
15 What time is it?

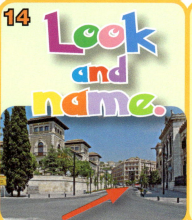
14 Look and name.

13 What can you see in a planetarium?

1 Read and find three mistakes.

This is me.
I was four years old.
I was at a bowling alley with my sister. It was winter. It was cold and rainy. My favorite toy was a teddy bear.

2 Look and write about Raquel's photo.

My name's Raquel. In this photo, I was six years old. I was at an …

3 Look and read. Say in pairs.

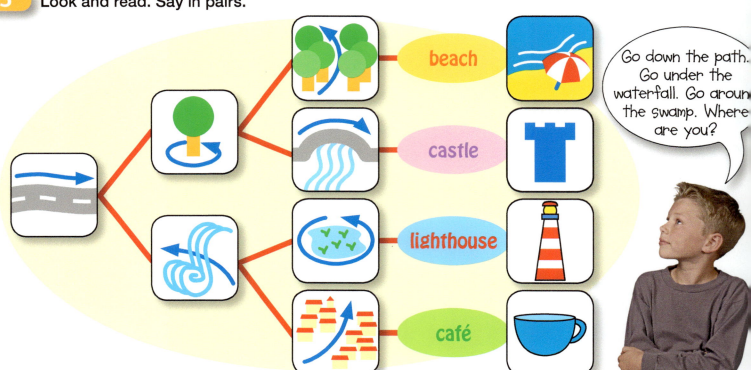

Go down the path. Go under the waterfall. Go around the swamp. Where are you?

4 Read and identify the place.

Where is it?

1 It's a very big house. Kings and queens live here.
2 You can see paintings and sculptures here.
3 There are dolphins, octopuses and jellyfish, but it isn't the ocean.
4 It's a good place to learn about the Moon, planets and stars.
5 There are lots of cameras and lights. Actors work here.
6 It's cold and dark. Bats live here.
7 There are lots of houses and stores here.
8 It's cold. You can go skating on the ice.

Contents

0	Hello!	2
1	Home Time	3
2	Kids can cook!	5
3	Staying Healthy	7
4	Let's go shopping!	9
5	Ocean Life	11
6	Wonderful World	13
7	A great day!	15
8	Adventure Island	17

Picture Dictionary	19
Beep on Grammar	27
Track List	35

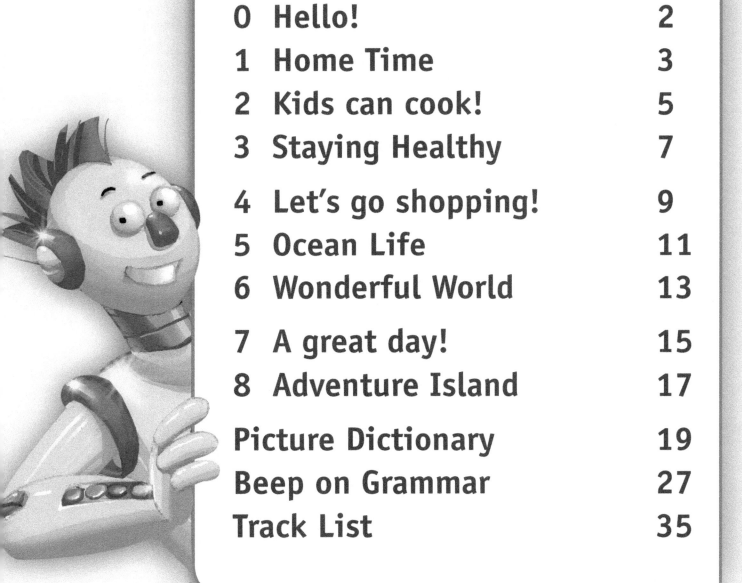

Hello!

1 Write in order. Then look in the Student's Book and write the name.

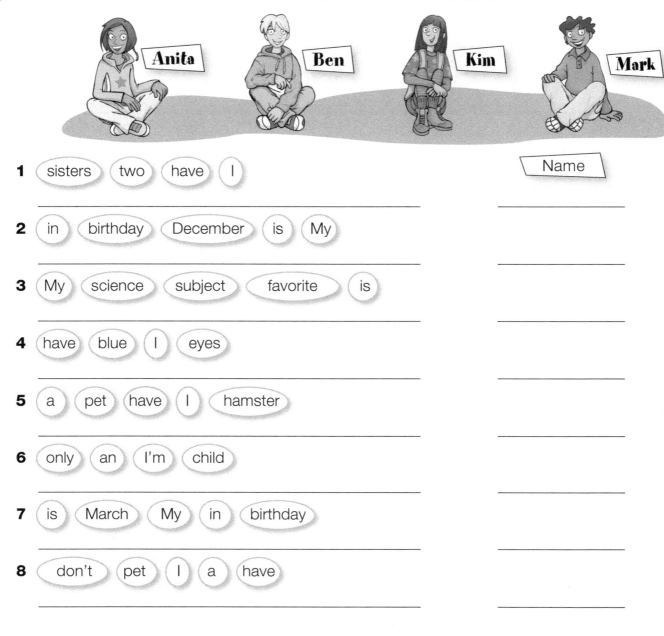

1. (sisters) (two) (have) (I)
   _____   Name _____

2. (in) (birthday) (December) (is) (My)
   _____   _____

3. (My) (science) (subject) (favorite) (is)
   _____   _____

4. (have) (blue) (I) (eyes)
   _____   _____

5. (a) (pet) (have) (I) (hamster)
   _____   _____

6. (only) (an) (I'm) (child)
   _____   _____

7. (is) (March) (My) (in) (birthday)
   _____   _____

8. (don't) (pet) (I) (a) (have)
   _____   _____

2 Complete your profile. Then write sentences.

Student Profile
Name: _____
Family: _____
Eyes: _____
Birthday: _____
Pets: _____
Favorite subject: _____

My name is _____
_____
_____
_____
_____

1. Home Time

1 Look at the chart, then listen and complete.

	never	sometimes	usually	always

1. Do you read in bed?   I always read in bed.
2. Do you do the dishes?   _____
3. Do you watch TV?   _____
4. Do you practice the guitar?   _____
5. Do you listen to music?   _____
6. Do you walk the dog?   _____

2 Write the words in order and circle according to your routines.

1. (at) (have) (o'clock) (you) (dinner) (six) (Do)
_____?   Yes, I do.   No, I don't.

2. (computer) (play) (Do) (games) (you)
_____?   Yes, I do.   No, I don't.

3. (Do) (bed) (you) (read) (in)
_____?   Yes, I do.   No, I don't.

4. (music) (Do) (to) (you) (listen)
_____?   Yes, I do.   No, I don't.

3 Read about Tim. Then write about you.

Hello, I'm Tim. On Saturdays, I always play computer games and see my friends. I usually read books and watch TV. I sometimes play the recorder and go to the movies. I never play basketball.

_____
_____
_____
_____
_____

Review

1 Look, circle and write.

(do) go see play (the) to my bed the friends dishes recorder

do the _____ | _____ | _____ | _____

2 Read and complete the questions.

Do you _____ TV?

No, I never watch TV.

What time _____ _____ have dinner?

I always have dinner at seven thirty.

_____ _____ do the dishes?

Yes, I sometimes do the dishes.

3 Write about your Sundays.

always
usually
sometimes
never

I _____ do my homework.
I _____ clean my room.
I _____ go to the park.
I _____ go to school.
I sometimes _____ .
I usually _____ .

Sunday

2. Kids can cook!

1 Listen and check (✓) or cross (✗).

2 Look at Activity 1 and complete the speech bubbles.

- I don't have any spaghetti.
- _____ chicken.
- _____ chocolate.
- I have some hot dogs.
- _____ salad.
- _____ ice cream.

3 Read about Leo and complete.

bread   dinner   sister   lunch   have   summer   favorite   usually

Hello, I'm Leo. I'm from Ireland. I have breakfast with my _____. We always have eggs, _____ and apple juice. I have _____ at school at one o'clock. We usually _____ meat, pizza or pasta. At six thirty, I have _____ with my family. We _____ have salad or fish and vegetables. My _____ food is watermelon. I eat it every day in the _____.

Review

1 Write the food words and match.

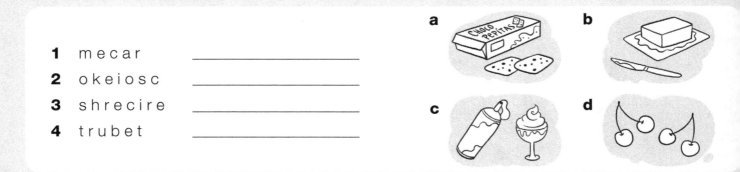

1 m e c a r _____
2 o k e i o s c _____
3 s h r e c i r e _____
4 t r u b e t _____

2 Look at the pictures and complete the dialogue.

1 Do __we have any__ sugar?

2 No, we don't, but we _____ _____ flour.

3 Good! Oh look, we _____ _____ any butter.

4 OK, we need _____ butter and _____ eggs, too.

5 Do we _____ _____ chocolate?

6 Yes, _____ _____ some chocolate.

3 Look, read and circle. Then draw the missing food in the bag.

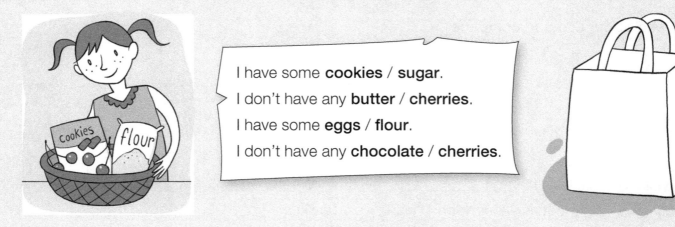

I have some **cookies** / **sugar**.
I don't have any **butter** / **cherries**.
I have some **eggs** / **flour**.
I don't have any **chocolate** / **cherries**.

3. Staying Healthy

1 Listen and match.

How often do you take a shower?

I take a shower every day.

1 How often do you take a shower?
2 How often do you eat salad?
3 How often do you drink juice?
4 How often do you sleep eight hours?
5 How often do you do exercise?
6 How often do you eat junk food?

a six times a week
b every day
c once a week
d twice a week
e three times a week
f five times a week

2 Look at Activity 1. Read and complete for Tim.

I _____ once a week.

I _____ twice a week.

I _____ three times a week.

I do exercise _____.

I sleep eight hours _____.

I take a shower _____.

3 Write in order and answer for you.

1 (watch) (How) (TV) (you) (often) (do)
_____? _____.

2 (do) (eight) (often) (you) (hours) (sleep) (How)
_____? _____.

3 (often) (do) (How) (eat) (you) (fruit)
_____? _____.

4 (exercise) (do) (you) (often) (How) (do)
_____? _____.

7

Review

1 Read and complete. Write the letter.

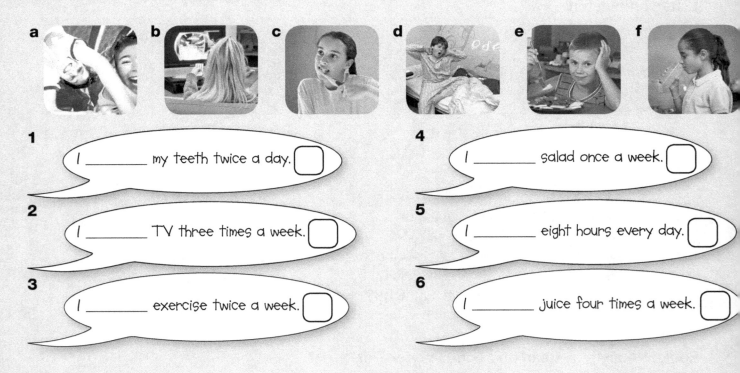

1 I _____ my teeth twice a day. ☐
2 I _____ TV three times a week. ☐
3 I _____ exercise twice a week. ☐
4 I _____ salad once a week. ☐
5 I _____ eight hours every day. ☐
6 I _____ juice four times a week. ☐

2 Complete the questions and answer for you.

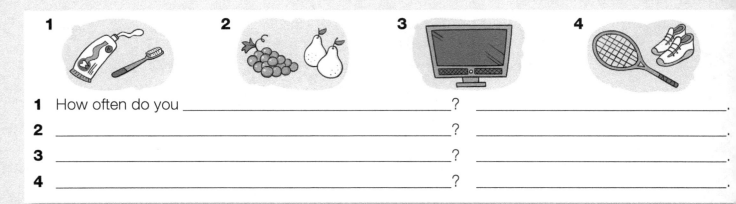

1 How often do you _____ ? _____.
2 _____ ? _____.
3 _____ ? _____.
4 _____ ? _____.

3 Look and write about Harry.

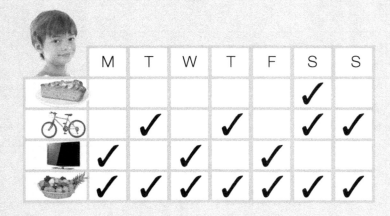

Harry eats _____ once a _____.
He _____ his bike _____ _____ _____.
He watches _____ _____ times _____.
_____ _____ _____ every _____.

4. Let's go shopping!

1 Look and write.

turn left
crosswalk
go straight
traffic lights
turn right

 1. _____
 2. _____

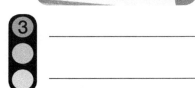 3. _____
 4. _____
 5. _____

2 Listen and number. 4.1

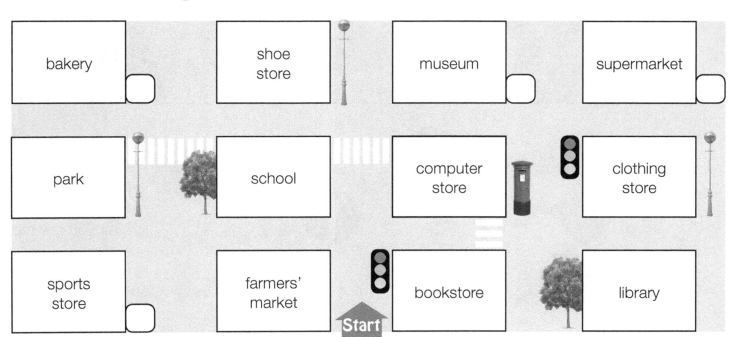

Review

1 Look and write the names of the stores.

2 Look at Activity 1 and complete the sentences.

1 The shoe store is _____ _____ the bakery.
2 The supermarket is _____ _____ the farmers' market.
3 The clothing store is _____ the supermarket and the computer store.
4 The _____ is across from the bookstore.

3 Look and complete the sentences.

Where's the computer store?

Cross at the crosswalk and _____. Go past the supermarket, then  _____. _____ until you see the school. _____ and it's next to the clothing store.

5. Ocean Life

1 Write the questions. Then listen and write the answers. 5.1

1 (live) (alone) (Do) (octopuses) _____ ? _____ .
2 (fish) (Do) (they) (eat) _____ ? _____ .
3 (they) (eat) (plants) (Do) _____ ? _____ .
4 (Do) (air) (they) (breathe) _____ ? _____ .
5 (eggs) (they) (Do) (lay) _____ ? _____ .

2 Write the sentences.

1 eBul leshaw ivel ni prugos _____
2 eyTh no'dt ayl gges _____
3 heyT thebrae rai _____
4 Tehy tea naplts _____

Which sentence is false? ☐

11

Review

1 Look and write the names of the animals.

1 _____ 2 _____ 3 _____ 4 _____ 5 _____ 6 _____

2 Read and complete. Then listen and check.

live / don't live   eat / don't eat   breathe / don't breathe

Great white sharks _____ fish.
They _____ air, because they have gills. They _____ alone.

Seals _____ in big groups. They don't have gills and they _____ air. They like eating fish. They _____ plants.

3 Look and write about turtles with *They have* or *They don't have.*

1 _____ gills.
2 _____ tails.
3 _____ flippers.
4 _____ dorsal fins.

12

6. Wonderful World

1 Listen and write the numbers.

6,960   910   6,650   8,848   6,300   3,404

Everest, Nepal
__8,848__ meters.

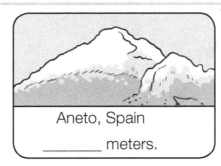

Aneto, Spain
_____ meters.

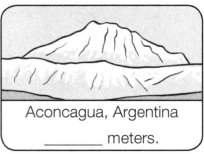

Aconcagua, Argentina
_____ meters.

Yangtze, China
_____ kilometers.

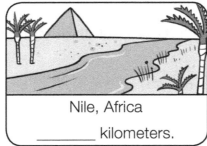

Nile, Africa
_____ kilometers.

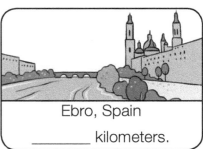

Ebro, Spain
_____ kilometers.

2 Look and write the numbers.

| seven
four
two | thousand | seven
five
six
two | hundred | ninety-five
eighty-two
forty-one
eighty-six |

2,582 = _____

4,795 = _____

641 = _____

7,286 = _____

3 Read and write the numbers.

Mount Kilimanjaro is in Africa. It's (5,895) _____
_____ meters high. Every year, (15,000) _____
_____ people climb Mount Kilimanjaro.
When it's sunny, you can see (120) _____
kilometers from the top. A lot of animals live on Mount Kilimanjaro. There are (179)
_____ species of birds.

Review

1 Look and label.

1 _____ 2 _____ 3 _____ 4 _____ 5 _____

2 Circle, then complete the sentences with the numbers.

Two ten thousand hundred seventy hundred one five hundred three eighty thousand nine hundred

A 6,425 = Six ___thousand___, four _____ twenty - _____.

B 10,186 = _____ thousand, _____ _____ _____ - six.

C 973 = nine _____ _____ - _____.

D 2,849 = _____ _____, eight _____ forty - _____.

3 Look at page 51 in the Student's Book. Use the information to write in order.

1 (than) (the Atlantic Ocean) (bigger) (The Pacific Ocean) (is)

_____

2 (longer) (The Nile River) (is) (than) (the Amazon River)

_____

3 (Teide) (Mont Blanc) (than) (higher) (is)

_____

4 (colder) (The South Pole) (than) (is) (the North Pole)

_____

14

7. A great day!

1 Write in order. Circle *True* or *False*.

When I Was Little

1 favorite toy a My was car
_____ True False

2 windy was It cold and
_____ True False

3 a My was toy plane favorite
_____ True False

4 was jacket My white
_____ True False

5 superhero a I was
_____ True False

2 Listen and circle the five mistakes. Then write the correct text below.

This is Miriam. She was at her first Christmas party. She was five years old. She was a giant. Her cat was black. It was cloudy and hot. Her favorite food was spaghetti.

windy   soup   Jane   Halloween   witch   six

This is Jane . She was _____
_____
_____ .

3 Answer for you.

1 What was your favorite toy?   My favorite toy was _____.
2 Who was your first teacher?   _____
3 What was your favorite place?   _____

15

Review

1 Circle the one that is different and write the letter.

1 fish   shell   crab   boat   ☐

2 cloud   planet   star   galaxy   ☐

3 queen   actor   throne   tiara   ☐

4 camera   actor   telescope   director   ☐

a
b
c
d

2 Look and write.

Jan's Busy Day

This is Jan. He was at the skating rink at ten o'clock. At twelve o'clock _____ _____ at the restaurant. After lunch _____ _____ at the _____ alley. At three o'clock _____ _____ at the _____. What a busy day!

3 Look and complete the sentences.

1 I was at the _____.

Where were you on Tuesday?

2 _____

3 _____

16

8. Adventure Island

1 Look and write.

go | along / under / through / over / around

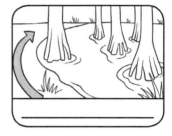
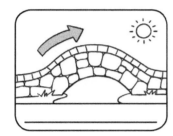
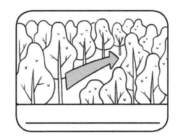
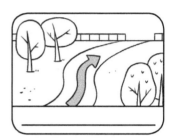

2 Listen and number the boxes.

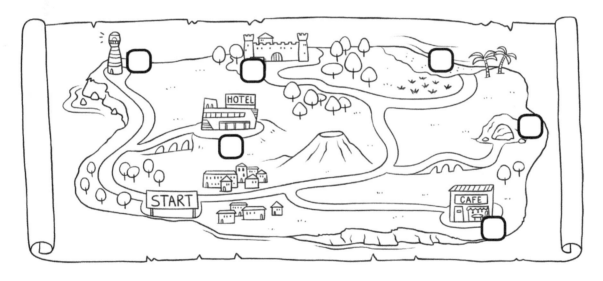

3 Look at Activity 2 and complete. Then write.

START Go _____ the town, go _____ the volcano. Go _____ the path, go _____ the forest. There's the castle!

START Go through the town. _____
_____
_____
_____. There's the beach!

17

Review

1 Look and label.

2 Look and write.

Go | under along through around over | the swamp the path the town the bridge the waterfall

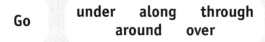

Start at the _____ . _____ _____ _____

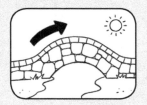  

_____ _____ Finish at the _____ .

3 Look and complete.

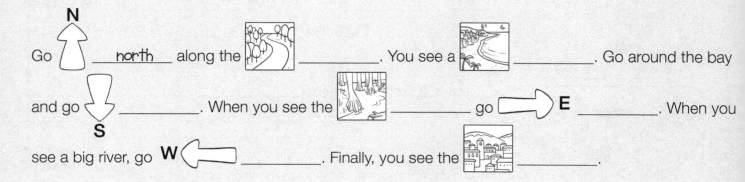

Go __north__ along the _____ . You see a _____ . Go around the bay and go _____ . When you see the _____ go _____ . When you see a big river, go _____ . Finally, you see the _____ .

18

Picture Dictionary 1

Write these words and phrases in your language.

 clean my room

_____

 have dinner

_____

 do my homework

_____

 play the recorder

_____

 do the dishes

_____

 see my friends

_____

 go to bed

_____

 walk the dog

_____

 always

_____

 sometimes

_____

 never

_____

 usually

_____

Picture Dictionary 2

Write these words in your language.

 butter

 cream

 cherries

 eggs

 chocolate

 flour

 cookies

 sugar

 add

 mix

 bake

 put

breakfast

lunch

dinner

Picture Dictionary 3

Write these words and phrases in your language.

 brush your teeth
_____

 eat junk food
_____

 do exercise
_____

 sleep eight hours
_____

 drink water
_____

 watch a lot of TV
_____

 eat healthy food
_____

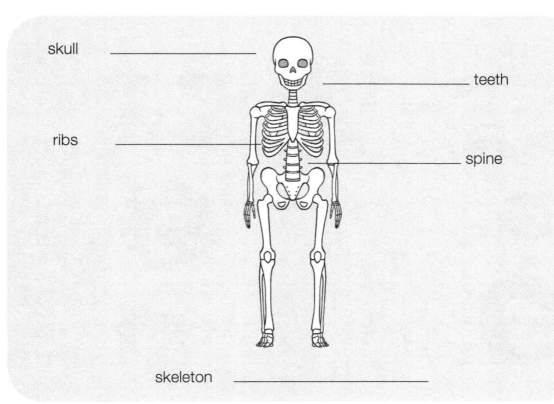

skull _____

teeth _____

ribs _____

spine _____

skeleton _____

Picture Dictionary 4

Write these words and phrases in your language.

 bakery
_____

 farmers' market
_____

 bookstore
_____

 shoe store
_____

 clothing store
_____

 sports store
_____

 computer store
_____

 supermarket
_____

 across from
_____

 next to
_____

 between
_____

 turn left
_____

 go straight
_____

 turn right
_____

Picture Dictionary 5

Write these words and phrases in your language.

 blue whale

 orca

 crab

 seal

 dolphin

 shark

 jellyfish

 starfish

 octopus

 turtle

 breathe air

 have babies

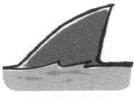 dorsal fin

 gills

 flippers

 tentacles

Picture Dictionary 6

Write these words and phrases in your language.

 a dry **desert**
_____

 a high **mountain**
_____

 a big **forest**
_____

 a wide **ocean**
_____

 a small **island**
_____

 a long **river**
_____

 a deep **lake**
_____

 a hot **volcano**
_____

 clean
_____

 quiet
_____

 cold
_____

 sunny
_____

 cloudy
_____

 windy
_____

 noisy
_____

two thousand _____    five hundred _____   meters _____   kilometers _____

24

Picture Dictionary 7

Write these words and phrases in your language.

 amusement park
_____

 movie studio
_____

 aquarium
_____

 planetarium
_____

 bowling alley
_____

 skating rink
_____

 gallery
_____

 palace
_____

07:45 It's quarter to eight.
_____

03:30 It's three thirty.
_____

01:35 It's twenty-five to two.
_____

09:20 It's twenty after nine.
_____

25

Picture Dictionary 8

Write these words and phrases in your language.

bridge _____ 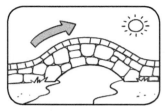 go over _____

forest _____  go through _____

path _____  go along _____

swamp _____  go around _____

waterfall _____  go under _____

 bay _____

 cave _____

 cliff _____

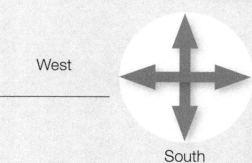 town _____

North _____

West _____

East _____

South _____

Beep on Grammar 1

| I | always
usually
sometimes
never | have dinner at seven o'clock.
play soccer on Saturday.
do the dishes.
go to school on Sunday. | always = ✓✓✓
usually = ✓✓
sometimes = ✓
never = ✗ |

Look and write.

| Saturday | walk the dog
✓✓✓ | do my homework
✓ | see my friends
✓✓ | play the guitar
✗ |

1. I always walk the dog on Saturday.
2. _____
3. _____
4. _____

Look and complete with *always, usually, sometimes, never*.

1. ✗ swim in the ocean
2. ✓✓ listen to music
3. ✓✓✓ swim in the ocean
4. ✓ go to bed at 10

_____   _____   _____   _____

It's eleven o'clock.   It's eight fifteen.   It's two thirty.   It's quarter to three.

Look and write the times.

1.
2.
3.
4.

It's _____   _____   _____   _____

Read and answer.

1. What time do you have breakfast?   I have breakfast at _____.
2. What time do you do your homework?   _____
3. What time do you have math on Monday?   _____
4. What time do you get up on Sunday?   _____

Beep on Grammar 2

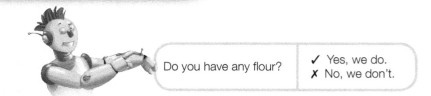

Do you have any flour?   ✓ Yes, we do.   ✗ No, we don't.

1 Look and write questions.

1  Do you have any flour? _____

2 _____

3 _____

4 _____

2 Look and answer.

1 Do we have any bananas?   4 Do we have any meat?
2 Do we have any peppers?   5 _____
3 Do we have any carrots?   _____ ?

1 No, we don't.   4 _____
2 _____   5 Yes, we do.
3 _____

We have | some | cookies.   We don't have | any | butter.

3 Look at the pictures and complete the sentences.

1 ____We____ have ___some___ chocolate.
2 We _____ have _____ sugar.
3 _____ don't have _____ cream.
4 _____ have _____ cherries.
5 _____ butter.
6 _____ cookies.

What do you have in your fridge?

We _____

_____

28

Beep on Grammar 3

| How often do you | brush your teeth?
take a shower?
drink juice? | once a week
three times a week | twice a week
every day |

Complete the questions and answer for you.

1 How _____ do you _eat_ junk food?

I eat junk food _____.

2 How _____ often _____ watch _____ ?

_____.

Complete for you.

1 _I go to school five times a week._
2 _____
3 _____
4 _____
5 _____

go to school ~~~ read books   do homework
use a computer   listen to music

| He
She | goes to the park
plays basketball | once a week.
four times a week. | twice a week.
every day. |

Look and write the times.

	once a week	three times a week
	five times a week	four times a week
	every day	five times a week
	three times a week	twice a week
	four times a week	every day

How often...

1 ...does Helen eat fruit? _She eats fruit five times a week._
2 ...does Bill listen to music? _____
3 ...does Helen play basketball? _____
4 ...does Bill ride a bike? _____
5 ...does Bill eat fruit? _____
6 ...does Helen drink juice? _____

29

Beep on Grammar 4

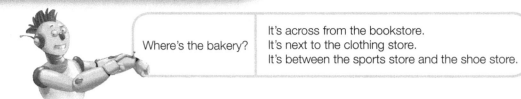

Where's the bakery? It's across from the bookstore.
It's next to the clothing store.
It's between the sports store and the shoe store.

1 Unscramble the sentences and write the store numbers in the boxes.

1 computer store / and / between / the / farmers' market / the / It's
_____
_____

2 next to / sports store / the / It's
_____
_____

3 the / It's / computer store / across from
_____
_____

2 Look at the stores and answer.

1 Where's the farmers' market? (next to) _____
2 Where's the computer store? (across from) _____
3 Where's the bakery? (between) _____

| I | love
really like
don't like
hate | novels.

joke books. | He
She | loves
really likes
doesn't like
hates | comic books.

ghost stories. |

3 Complete for you.

1 _____ information books.   2 _____ novels.

4 Look and write about April and Nico.

1 Nico _____ joke books.
2 April _____ comic books.
3 April _____ detective stories.
4 Nico _____ information books.

| love | really like | don't like | hate |

 April

  Nico

Beep on Grammar 5

Look at the pictures, complete the questions and answer.

Lay eggs	Eat plants	Live in groups	Breathe air

1 Do __seals__ lay __eggs__ ? __No, they don't.__
2 Do octopuses _____ eggs? _____
3 _____ seals _____ plants? _____
4 Do _____ _____ plants? _____

5 _____ seals _____ in groups? _____
6 Do _____ live _____ groups? _____
7 _____ octopuses _____ air? _____
8 Do _____ _____ air? _____

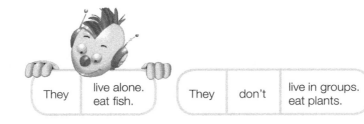

Look at Unit 5 in the Student's Book. Write in order and circle the correct animal.

eggs / don't / They / lay
1 _____

alone / live / They
2 _____

eat / They / turtles
3 _____

don't / fins / have / They
4 _____

have / They / babies
5 _____

Look and write about seahorses.

1 They don't eat plants.
2 _____
3 _____
4 _____

Seahorses			
eat plants	✗	live in groups	✓
breathe air	✗	lay eggs	✓

31

Beep on Grammar 6

8,954	eight		nine		fifty-four
17,436	seventeen	thousand,	four	hundred	thirty-six
2,671	two		six		seventy-one

1 Look at the chart and write the numbers.

three		two		twelve
ten	thousand,	five	hundred	forty-five
five		nine		sixty-seven

3,912 = _____

5,567 = _____

10,245 = _____

2 Look and complete.

1 Teide is ____three____ thousand, seven _____ _____ meters high.

2 The Danube River is two _____, eight _____ _____ kilometers long.

3 The Empire State Building is _____ _____ _____ meters high.

4 Everest is _____ _____, _____ _____ _____ meters high.

Teide
3,718 meters

Danube
2,872 kilometers

Empire State Building
443 meters

Everest
8,848 meters

The Nile River is	**longer**		the Amazon River.
Mount Everest is	**higher**	than	Mont Blanc.
Russia is	**bigger**		China.

3 Look, read and complete.

bigger   hotter   higher   longer

23° C   16° C

1 Barcelona is _____ than London.

8,611 m   4,810 m

2 K2 is _____ than Mont Blanc.

120,536 km   12,100 km

3 Saturn is _____ than Venus.

6,400 km   2,872 km

4 The Amazon River is _____ than the Danube River.

4 Finish the sentences.

1 I am taller than _____.

2 I am older _____.

3 A mouse is bigger _____.

Beep on Grammar 7

| I / He/She / It | was | at a gallery. / twelve. / hot and sunny. |

| How old / Where | were | you? |

Hugo

Write in order. Look at the picture and circle T (True) or F (False).

1 at / movie studio / Hugo / the / was
   _____ T F

2 sister / with / was / He / his
   _____ T F

3 winter / was / It
   _____ T F

4 sunny / It / cold / was / and
   _____ T F

Read and complete the dialogue.

| old   aquarium   Was   summer   grandma   were |

Gina: Look! This is me.
Adam: Where _____ you?
Gina: I was at the _____.
I was with my _____.

Adam: How _____ were you?
Gina: I was seven. It was my birthday.
Adam: _____ it cold?
Gina: No, it was hot. It was _____.

Gina

It's twenty to four.   It's five to six.   It's ten after six.   It's twenty-five after eleven.

Look and write the times.

1 _____   2 _____   3 _____

Look and complete the sentences about Katy.

| 9:20 | 2:40 | 3:10 | 8:55 |
| gallery | bowling alley | palace | movie studio |

1 At twenty to three, _Katy was at the bowling alley._
2 At ten after three, _____.
3 At twenty after nine, _____.
4 _____, Katy was at the movie studio.

33

Beep on Grammar 8

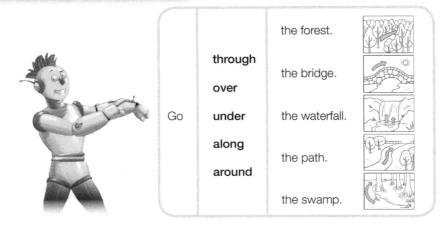

Go	through	the forest.
	over	the bridge.
	under	the waterfall.
	along	the path.
	around	the swamp.

1 Read and complete.

1. Start at the lighthouse. Go over the bridge. Go around the lake. Go one square north. Go through the small town. Where are you? _____
2. Start at the palace. Go around the swamp. Go north along the cliff. Go under the waterfall. Go one square west. Where are you? _____
3. Start at the beach. _____. Go around the lake. Go three squares south. Where are you? The big town!

2 Look and write the route.

> The lighthouse to the hotel.

_____
_____
_____

Track List

Student's Book
Songs, chants and stories

Track	Transcript	
Unit 0		
1	0.2	Song: Things I like to do
Unit 1		
2	1.1	Song: Home Time!
3	1.4	The Science Project!
4	1.5	Chant: My Day!
5	1.6	The Adventures of Beep!
Unit 2		
6	2.1	Song: Kids can cook!
7	2.4	Story: Kids Start Cooking!
8	2.5	Song: The TV Chef Rap!
9	2.6	The Adventures of Beep!
Unit 3		
10	3.1	Song: The Healthy Song!
11	3.3	Story: Kay's Big Race!
12	3.4	Chant: Some things are good.
13	3.6	The Adventures of Beep!
Unit 4		
14	4.1	Song: We're going shopping!
15	4.5	Story: A Day in London!
16	4.6	Chant: Where's the bookstore?
17	4.7	The Adventures of Beep!
Unit 5		
18	5.1	Song: We're going to the aquarium!
19	5.4	Story: The Shipwreck!
20	5.6	Song: The Song of the Great Blue Whale!
21	5.7	The Adventures of Beep!
Unit 6		
22	6.1	Song: Look at our world!
23	6.5	Story: A Long Way to School!
24	6.6	Chant: My Village in the Mountains!
25	6.7	The Adventures of Beep!

Track	Transcript	
Unit 7		
26	7.1	Song: I love going out with my family!
27	7.4	Story: Robbery at the Palace!
28	7.5	Chant: Where were you?
29	7.6	The Adventures of Beep!
Unit 8		
30	8.1	Song: Adventure Island!
31	8.4	Story: The Secret of Blackbeard's Bay!
32	8.5	Chant: North, South, East, West!
33	8.7	The Adventures of Beep!

Activity Book
Exercises

Track	Transcript	
34	1.1	Look at the chart then listen and complete.
35	2.1	Listen and check (✓) or cross (✗).
36	3.1	Listen and match.
37	4.1	Listen and number.
38	5.1	Write the questions. Then listen and write the answers.
39	5.2	Read and complete. Then listen and check.
40	6.1	Listen and write the numbers.
41	7.1	Listen and circle the five mistakes. Then write the correct text below.
42	8.1	Listen and number the boxes.

Picture Dictionary

43	PD1	Picture Dictionary 1
44	PD2	Picture Dictionary 2
45	PD3	Picture Dictionary 3
46	PD4	Picture Dictionary 4
47	PD5	Picture Dictionary 5
48	PD6	Picture Dictionary 6
49	PD7	Picture Dictionary 7
50	PD8	Picture Dictionary 8